TARA GARDNER

Happy Little Trees

A Memoir of Trauma, Dissociation, and Healing

First edition

This book was professionally typeset on Reedsy.
Find out more at reedsy.com

To the girl who felt lost in the shadows, unsure of her worth and her path. This is for you, for your strength in the face of adversity, for the courage you found to keep going even when the way seemed dark. May these pages serve as a testament to your resilience and as a reminder that every struggle was a step towards becoming the woman you are today. Thank you for holding on. I'll take it from here.

Contents

Acknowledgments iii
Introduction 1

I Cracks in the Foundation

1 The Girl in the Window 5
2 And Then There Was One 16
3 Coloring Outside the Lines 19
4 The Art Contest 22
5 Permission to LOL 26
6 Sister Sister 28
7 Added Weight 31
8 Out of Reach 35
9 Georgia Bound 37
10 Daddy issues 42

II The Lost Pieces

11 Out of Place 49
12 Look Both Ways 52
13 Sorry Not Sorry 55
14 Funny Tape 58
15 The Constant 61
16 Hollow Years 66

17 Love in Measure 68
18 Motherhood 71
19 The Rabbit Hole 74
20 Piecing Me Together 77

III The Road to Wholeness

21 Dear Little me 81
22 When Worlds Collide 83
23 Good Grief 88
24 Where Healing Begins 94
25 Boundaries and Grace 96
26 Triggers & Transformation 100
27 My Superpower 103
28 Acceptance 105

About the Author 107

Acknowledgments

I want to extend my deepest gratitude to my therapist, Dr. D., whose insight and guidance were pivotal in my healing journey. Your wisdom and compassion helped me navigate the darkest moments of my life and find the strength to reclaim my story. Thank you for helping me see the truth and for being a steadfast source of support.

Introduction

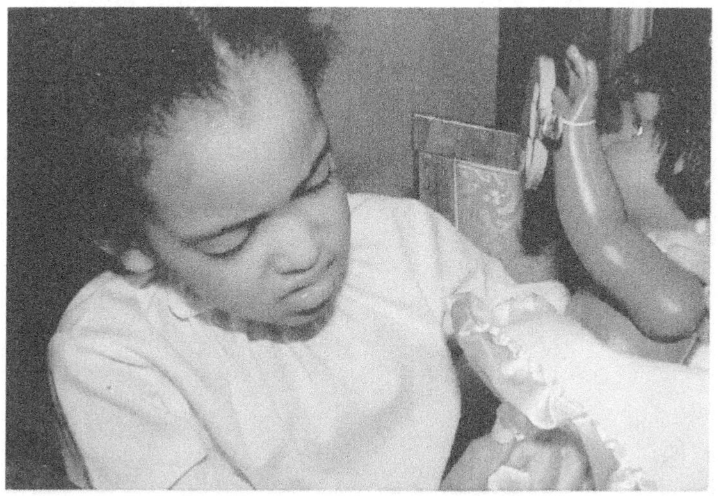

The girl behind these words

"Tara, you think you are protecting that little girl, but that little girl is the one calling the shots!" My therapist's words echoed in my mind long after our session ended. For years, I had believed I was shielding the fragile child within me, never realizing she was the one dictating my every move. It was a revelation that turned my world upside down, forcing me to confront the fears and behaviors that had controlled my life.

This is the journey of how I faced that inner child, found healing through faith and motherhood, and transformed my pain into a purpose-driven life.

I titled this book *Happy Little Trees* after a quote from Bob Ross: *"Anything we don't like, we'll turn it into a happy little tree or something."* I watched Bob Ross for years as a child, completely absorbed in his shows, and his gentle voice and perspective stayed with me. Just like he painted his trees with patience, care, and a sense of peace, I've learned to face the pieces of my own life with intention, faith, and a willingness to grow.

Thank you for reading my story.

I

Cracks in the Foundation

1

The Girl in the Window

I was about three years old and I lived in a house in Brooklyn with my mom, my big sister, a couple of aunts, some cousins, my grandmother and a few others here and there. It was a full house and there was never a dull moment.

One of my cousins and I were practically joined at the hip and we did almost everything together. We would play make believe, skate, build forts and play with dolls. You know, what kids do. We spent a lot of time with our grandmother. She would watch us while our moms were at work. She sat in her chair most of the day, smoking Winston 100 cigarettes and watching Channel 2 Soap Operas.

After the Soaps she would make us Cornmeal Porridge or soft boiled eggs we'd eat from the shell, and she had it ready in just enough time for her to watch *The Price is Right*. She would tell us stories about growing up in Jamaica, about all the different relatives, many whom I've never met and many who I'd meet later in life.

She repeated the same stories over and over but we always let her finish because well, she was Grandma and she had the right. And to her credit, her stories were always interesting, even the tenth time around. We had a lot of fun in that house, for a while anyway. Then before I knew it, my mom moved me and my sister to an Apartment in Crown Heights.

When we moved to Crown Heights, Lauren and I shared a room with bunk beds. Lauren slept on the bottom bunk and I was on the top. Lauren had the biggest eyes and she often slept with her eyes open and her eyes rolled back so you could only see the white. If I had to leave my bunk for anything at night, I made it a point not to look her way or I might not make it back to sleep that night. It didn't take much to scare me.

Very soon after moving there, late one night Lauren and I were woken up by commotion. We rushed to the living room and sat up on the couch which faced the kitchen. The kitchen had old linoleum flooring and on the other side of the kitchen was an entrance to a long dark hallway to the right which led to the front door. My mom came around the corner toward the hallway. A man followed her. He carried a large leather suitcase and a few other bags.

"This is Luther," she said. He nodded once. That was it. I remember thinking we just moved so we could finally have my mom to ourselves. Instead, suddenly, I felt like the stranger.

Soon, I no longer had the access I once had to my mother. I was too clingy. If I needed my mom in the middle of the night, her bedroom door was locked. Things were just different.

On my first day of school I was torn between excited and scared. We were brought to a large courtyard of the school early in the morning and parents were to put us in a line according to age and birth date which would determine what class we were in. I remember a lady asking my mother how old I was and she held my hand tight and told the lady I was 5. The lady directed her to place me at the end of one of the many lines formed in the courtyard, The first grade line. She said "Stay in this line and follow them. I'll be back for you later, okay?"

I knew I was 4 years old and never said anything because back then you spoke when you were spoken to, and I wasn't going to correct my mom, especially in front of another adult. I just did what I was told.

Halfway through the school year, I was called to the office with my mom and they were discussing how I was supposed to be in kindergarten because of my age. My mom politely challenged the rule by asking how I was doing in first grade. My teacher, Ms. Silver... I loved Ms. Silver, argued that I was doing exceptionally well and should be given a chance to stay and they let me stay.

I always figured my real age just slipped my mother's mind that day as an unimportant detail from the many things she was juggling. It wasn't until very recent that I learned she lied on purpose because she knew my abilities. I found such a jolt of value in learning that piece of information about how my mom saw me at that very young age. My mom and I were so close back then. All of that changed when our step father moved in.

When Luther came to live there... he changed the air. It was cold, stifling. It was quiet other than the sound of his voice. His voice was so loud, it shook my heart when he so much as laughed. He even whispered loudly.

He would spend hours and hours reading the bible and preaching to us about what scriptures meant, highlighting verses, rewriting verses. He made sure we all had a bible and we would sit there for hours and hours. I remember sitting at the table with him for hours and the only sound was his voice. My mom would occasionally meekly interrupt and say, Luther, they need a break, they need to eat.

She would make us lunch. I liked when she would make me a tomato and cheese sandwich with wheat toast and margarine and hot cocoa made with soy milk. We were vegetarian per his instruction. Cows milk was also forbidden but I remember my mom still bought us cheese. He eventually went to a full raw foods regimen. I guess my mom let him know he could do that by his darn self cuz we eats! I would eat slow and hope she could distract him long enough to where he would not want to resume the lesson afterwards. It felt like being in a cage.

He would preach to us that people with blond hair and blue eyes were not of God's people. He would write pages and pages of his messages and his doctrine based on the etymology of words. He obsessed about Etymology and started to create language that omitted all vowels other than the vowel E. All the other vowels were not of the Holy language. Soon the letter S was not allowed because it sounded like a serpent. C sounded similar to S in some words so that letter was removed. Z was acceptable and replaced those consonants. All of these changes meant we could no longer be called the names we were given and we would now be renamed according to the new language, His new name was LETEHERE, My name was TERE, my mom, Patrice, was now PETEREZE, and so on and so on, for everyone in the home.

He believed he was a Prophet and even had followers who would come and sit with him for hours to hear him preach and discuss his doctrine. He would have us help him put together thick booklets of his teachings for his followers to distribute. The front page was bright highlighter gold colored and he would neatly hinge with a heavy duty stapler and use black masking tape to cover the stapled area to give them a neat finish. He recognized early, that I had great attention to detail and worked pretty fast. This pleased him and if I was busy doing that, I was at least occupied with something that would keep me awake while he preached.

It was annoying having people over all the time but it distracted him from us which I appreciated. He found me to be very smart and would occasionally call me in around his friends or followers just to ask me a question and impress them with my answer.

Later the letter E was dropped and the only acceptable vowel was I. He would write chants that we all had to say at a certain time of the day facing a certain direction, multiple times a day.

The chants were something like:

I, I

I, I

Most High I, I... and so on and so on, until we were released.

He would parade the streets chanting and preaching for all to hear. I was so embarrassed and never made it noticeable that we were related in any way. But people knew who he was, because many knew my mom.

Sometimes he would pray and chant on the roof of our apartment building. He started taking me to the roof of with him on the weekend mornings, I guess because I didn't have school. I didn't want to go. But I didn't have a choice. I was extremely afraid of heights. I tried to stay as far back as I could from the edge without drawing attention to my fear.

He would chant to the sky and one day when he was done, he looked over the edge and pointed something out. I couldn't make out what he was saying I was too afraid to concentrate. Then the words became clear, I guess because I had not responded to him. "Do you see it?" he asked, pointing downward.

My voice trembling, I said "not really, but its okay". I could see in that moment he saw the fear in me and he said. "Come look". I froze and shook my head as if to say, it's okay, I'm good. He very sternly said "come!" I inched forward, not to upset him and he began to lift me up.

As he lifted me up I left myself. He held me over the side of the roof and pointed out what he wanted to show me and I to this day don't know what it was. I was frozen like a log. He placed me back down and my legs were shaking. As my feet were reconnected to the rooftop, I came back to myself. My legs were trembling, I was numb and I could feel the blood rush to my head, but I did not cry. I just wanted this to be over and we headed back down to the apartment. I never said anything to anyone. I just figured I was a scaredy-cat and I needed to get it together.

Everything was his way. Nothing was neat enough or clean enough or said right enough. Brush your teeth this way! Read the bible... Clean this way! Pray this way! Eat this way! Say these words! This is your name! This is your mother's name! Like this! like this! like this!!!

At first it took a while to get used to doing things the "right" way. Tired of getting whipped on my hands and wrists with thick leather straps for not dusting off the TV that was never on, while my mom stood by and did nothing. She would just run my hands under cold water afterwards.

I knew I would have to get my act together soon or things would be worse. I learned the right way. The right things to say. The right things to do. What would impress him. I did all I could to please him because I just wanted to be at peace. Lauren hated this about me. I was a trader to her. But I had no choice. When she was gone there was only me. She was much older and had friends, outlets and temporary escapes to freedom that I could not count on.

Lauren was very vocal about her disgust with how our lives had changed so abruptly. Part of me thought she was brave. She told anyone who would listen what was happening in our home. She argued with Luther day in and day out about what she would and would not eat, what she would and would not do. My mom tried to diffuse it. She spoke softly. She pleaded, sometimes until hear face turned red. It didn't matter. It went on and on.

Lauren had a huge collection of stuffed animals. I can't even tell you how many, there were a lot. She loved them. I loved them too, even if I wasn't allow to touch them. One day, Luther gathered every single one of them and stuffed them into large black garbage bags. He threw them all away. I only remember bits and pieces. I remember Lauren crying, screaming. One of our aunts, who lived across the courtyard, went downstairs to try to salvage what she could. But where would it go?

Lauren also had artwork hanging on the wall of our bedroom. A poster board of a poem she wrote about love and what it meant to her, with a drawing of an angel, hearts, something soft and hopeful. He threw that away too.

He said he was removing all "graven images" from the home, that they were not of God. He even threw away his own jewelry. When I first met him, he wore a lot of it, gold chains, gold rings. Back then he reminded me of Mr. T, just without the Mohawk. None of it mattered anymore.

Lauren pushed back even harder after that, questioning, debating, refusing where she could. Most of it landed on deaf ears. I learned to stay quiet. Her resistance made her a problem. My obedience made me safe. At least for the moment.

There were pockets of moments where he wasn't all bad. He was very clean. He could be silly at times. He would take us to the park sometimes. But the ice was always very thin. Once he took me to the park and I started to swing. He taught me how to maneuver my legs to get more lift from the swing.

I found a comfortable height and was actually having a good time. Then he said "go higher". I smiled, tense, I said "I'm fine, I don't like to go too high". He started to push me on the swing higher and higher. I was scared and yelled "that's enough, that's too high!". I was clearly scared and near tears but I held them in. He continued to push me higher and higher, so high I thought the swing would loop over the top. I just closed my eyes, held on tight and held my breath. I didn't make a sound for the next few swings. I think maybe my silence made him wonder if I was okay and that made him stop.

Once the swing slowed down enough for me to break with my feet I jumped off of the swing. My legs were trembling. I found my breath and told him I really needed to use the bathroom so he would take me home and he did.

The anxiety that came from wondering what would upset or disappoint him, or just what would happen wasn't worth it. An uneventful day, preferably with very little interaction, was a good one.

There was a single bed in our bedroom that sat underneath the window. When I had moments to myself, I would sit at the window and just stare. There wasn't much to see out there, There were some old brick buildings and trees in the distance. Some of the buildings looked abandoned. I never saw people. I was too high up and there was too much clutter.

I was drawn to this old abandoned red brick building. I began to imagine that that building was filled with ghosts and skeletons and demons and that they knew I existed but that I was safe where I was, here in my room.

I would stare for what seemed like hours, in my wonderland. My mom would come in to check on me in the evening and bring me dinner. She would always put a handful of watercress greens on my plate knowing how much I hated them. "Eat them up" she'd say. "They're good for you." This would happen over and over.

Every now and then I would give it a taste to see if either my tolerance had grown or they magically tasted better than before. It was just horrible and bitter. I started throwing them out the window with a prayer that it would bless some appreciative animal, hoping a watercress tree did not start to grow one day, ratting me out.

My mom could cook! She made almost anything taste good but she was not subtle or creative when it came to getting us to eat healthy things we didn't like. When I was much younger, she would try to hide carrots in a spoonful of buttery rice. It was awful expecting something tasty and getting something else. Ugh! All I wanted was a choice.

From then on she would try to feed me and I would stick my finger in the spoon to check for unapproved ingredients. That would irritate her because it got messy. I think she sometimes found it funny and tried to hide her laughter and eventually gave up. Till this day I do not like people feeding me. This is one of my biggest pet peeves.

In a home where everything was his way, I learned quickly that surviving sometimes meant shrinking, hiding, or finding secret spaces for myself. All of this, the rules, the fear, the constant push and pull, became my everyday and yet, some parts of my life were about to change in ways I couldn't prepare for.

Because no matter how tightly I tried to hold myself together, the people closest to me, the ones I thought I could count on, had their own battles to fight. And sometimes, that meant I had to grow up faster than I was ready for. That's where Lauren came in, taking on a role I never asked for, but one I was about to lean on more than I knew.

2

And Then There Was One

One day, sitting on the lower bunk with the door closed, I could hear muffled voices and shuffling noises coming from living room Lauren was leaving.

She wouldn't fake getting along with our step dad. Neither of us liked him. I lived to survive though, try not to stir the waters. She preferred the battle approach. Well, in battle, sometimes there are casualties.

Eventually he gave my mom an ultimatum. She goes or he goes. So on this evening, just after the Sun went down. Our dad... Whom I referred to back then as Her dad, was coming to pick her up for good. I couldn't understand what happening or why. I didn't have all details at the time.

My mom had already "left". She was still "there" when he wasn't there, but he usually was. so eventually, I just let go. All I knew now was, all I had left, the closest thing to me, whether we got along all time or not, was being ripped away.

I walked down all those stairs behind her. She was carrying a big suitcase and I remember thinking it was big enough to fit me inside. I don't remember one word spoken the whole way down. Once she opened the lobby door to the outside, I remember the air hitting my face. It was a different air. It was like a reminder for me to breathe and exhale. "This is really happening" I thought to myself. I saw this car pull up and "dad" greeted me from the car. All I could acknowledge was her leaving. She turned to me and said goodbye and told me she would see me real soon.

At that moment my head filled with lava. I ran as fast as I could before a tear could hit the ground, back in the building, back up the stairs. Back to my room, our room, to the bottom bunk, her bunk. Bawling uncontrollably.

For a moment, I just knew one of them would follow me, to console me or at least try. But it was wishful thinking. My mom came in to console me. Her hand on my back meant to calm me, felt like sand paper against raw skin. Her concerned voice, sounded like hornets around my head. I cried myself to sleep that night.

I didn't know it then, but losing her, my closest ally, would leave cracks in the foundation I'd carry for years to come.

I hated being there alone with him. My mom would go to work and I would stay in my room afraid to breathe too hard. He knew I liked when my mom made me hot chocolate so he would attempt. How one makes hot chocolate taste like dirt is still a mystery to me. He did nothing the same as her. I just wanted my mom.

The hours in the day went by so slowly. When I heard her finally come home from work in the evenings I could finally exhale again. She would pretty much drop her purse where she stood and get right to cooking dinner. I'd be joined to her hip in the kitchen. It was the one moment I didn't have to compete for her time. I still had this part of her.

It would be months before Lauren returned. My mom had apparently been miserable without her, and Luther, in his own way, decided she should come back. If I'm honest, it was good to have her back, but I barely remember it. By then, she could have been anyone, really, just there to absorb some of the negative space with me.

3

Coloring Outside the Lines

Life at home pushed me toward the one place where I could escape, even if just for a little while: school. I was careful to keep my worlds separate, but school had its own rules, its own challenges, and its own tiny windows of freedom that I had to discover for myself.

First grade was awesome. I was learning new things everyday. I had the sweetest teacher, Ms. Silver. She was an older pudgy white lady with very short gray hair and the softest, most pleasant voice that encouraged us each day. I never saw her upset. I don't remember anything about first grade I did not like. School was great.

When we were promoted to second grade and I learned I would have a new teacher, I was really sad. My second grade teacher, Ms. Chenensky was a slightly younger white lady with short puffy blond hair. She had very thin lips and often wore hot pink lipstick. She was a great teacher, but she was less sweet and very strict. I remember being nervous in her class a lot. She did not tolerate talking in class. I used to nervously chew on the end of a blue and white Bic pen until it was almost unrecognizable.

I started to draw from the time I could pic up a pencil. I would draw flowers and people. I was about 4 years old when learned I had a gift. Once as I sat in the living room floor of my Grandma's apartment doodling her profile while she sat at her dining table, watching television, my aunt walked by and hovered over me for a second. Then quickly snatched the paper out of my hand. She stared at it in awe and said "my God Tara you drew this?"

"Mama look at this!" she said, showing my grandma the doodle I drew of her. Grandma looked and said "yes mi see-ar, is suh she sit and draw all dih while." (Translation: *yep, she does this all day long.*) Then Aunt Jasmine said to me, Tara-Lee!! That's another nickname she had for me outside of her "pet". "You can really draw! Keep it up Tara-Lee. You're so special." She handed me back the picture and I looked at it and then looked back at my grandma and thought to myself, I just drew what I saw. I figured this wasn't just something I like to do, it's special.

I remember often drawing naked bodies, men and women. I would doodle them and I felt things I could not explain. I also knew it was wrong, or that I shouldn't be doing it so I would destroy them so no one would find out.

One day, Sitting in my second grade class, my teacher picked up a sheet of paper from the floor and her facial expression changed. She appeared to be shocked. It was an 8 & 1/2 sheet of paper torn from a composition book that had a drawing of an anatomically correct woman and man. It was one of mine.

It was a pretty detailed drawing for a second grader. I was so nervous that she would know it was me. Fortunately, no one knew I was capable at that time. Ms. Chenensky held the drawing up briefly and frantically asking "who drew this?!" Kids in class looked around, some with their eyes popped out of their heads some with their hands over their mouths some with their hands over their eyes.

I was so scared, chewing on the end of my Bic pen like it was my final meal before death. I gasped and accidentally swallowed the end cap and now I was scared of what would happen, now I was not only praying that I wouldn't get caught, but that I would not die from swallowing a piece of plastic. No one knew it was me. I couldn't believe I was so careless not to destroy that picture. I had to be more careful and stop doing this bad thing.

School was one of the few places where I could just exist, quietly, without tiptoeing around anyone's moods. And when art entered the picture, it felt like a secret doorway opened just for me. It was during these small escapes, moments when I could breathe, focus, and create, that I found something I could call my own. Drawing and painting weren't just hobbies; they were lifelines, little pieces of me I could protect even when the rest of my world felt out of control.

4

The Art Contest

I did love to draw. It was so peaceful to me. I felt whole and useful when I would draw or paint. In third and fourth grade we would have an art teacher that came in a few days a week for an hour to teach us art. These were the best hours of my life.

My teacher was a young, tall slender white lady with long, strait brown hair down to her back. Ms. Lamb. I loved Ms. Lamb! She spoke my language. As they say today, she was a vibe. She saw something in me that was valuable and she never failed to express it.

I was still very shy and I never spoke about home in school. Very few things were acceptable at home so even when we had school trips, I rarely brought the permission slip to my mom to sign. I determined whether this would be acceptable to my mom based on Luther's new doctrine, or not and usually it wouldn't have been.

Museums... too much pagan history and white people, Movies...

too much exposure to ungodly things and white people, Pumpkin patch.... All about white people supporting Halloween. I got really good, really soon at forging my mom's signature. If I wanted to go on a school trip, I was going! If I needed money, I made up a reason to my mom to get it and that was that. She rarely challenged it. We didn't ask for much so she pretty much gave us what we asked for when we did. I think that was her way of compensating what I endured.

One week, Ms. Lamb had us paint pictures we chose from photographs she brought into class. I chose to paint Erasmus High School. We worked on that painting all week. It was the most detailed painting I remember doing at the time. The following week, she handed most of the student's paintings back to them to take home and she kept a few really good ones to hang up.

Mine was not handed back to me and it wasn't hanging up either. I was a little confused and kind of sad but I didn't say anything. As she handed out the last painting she looked right at me looking at her empty hands, I could see she noticed my disappointment. She headed toward me, and another teacher asked her a question drawing her attention away for a moment. As she spoke with him, she placed her hand on my shoulder as if to say, "*just a moment honey*".

Ms. Lamb was very likable but we only had her for an hour each day so there was never much time for any one on one moments. Once the other teacher left, she stooped down near my desk and said "Tara", and she reached out, held my face in her hands and smiled so big. This was new so I just nervously smiled back and waited. She told me my painting was exceptional and that she's sorry she didn't ask first, but that she entered my painting into a Nationwide Art contest and time was limited for entry.

My eyes opened so wide. I thought, wow me?! She went on to say the competition would be held in NYC and my parent would need to bring me. All I saw was my two worlds colliding in my head. This would mean I needed real approval. How would I get there? Could I tell my mom? Who could I get to play my mom? Would they support me? I went home that day and I nervously told my mom and she seemed so proud and happy. She asked me when it would take place and scheduled to take off of work that day. My mom Never took a day off of work! This was a big deal.

A couple of weeks went by and the date was near. The competition would be held on a Friday. On this particular Friday we learned that the one and only Whitney Houston would be performing at our little school. Whitney!! I loved me some Whitney Houston. I knew I would have to make a decision. It was surprisingly not hard to decide. I was going to that Art contest. I told myself, the chances of seeing Whitney changing my life was slim. So I went to the contest.

I think I came in 3rd in my division and brought home a big gold Trophy with my name engraved on it, along with the name of the competition, my division and placement. I was on cloud nine. I was so excited. My mom put the trophy in her bedroom on her dresser and I remember that Sunday I ran in her room to admire it again before going to bed.

The next day I went to school so excited. The principal announced my win on the loud speaker for the whole school to hear. It was a weird mixed feeling of *please no one look at me* and *look what I did.*

That day after school I rushed home and headed straight to my mom's room. I glanced on top of her dresser to get a glimpse of my trophy again but I didn't see it. So I went to my room to see if it was put in there but it wasn't. I went back to my mom's room and looked closer. I saw the bottom of the trophy that held the plaque with my name on it but the gold trophy that sat on top was gone. I was shattered. I just froze wondering why. What happened? This clearly was not an accident.

My mom later explained to me that Luther said the leaves and vines engraved on the trophy were sacrilegious because the bible clearly states that man should have no graven images. I didn't see this one coming. "I missed the vines" I thought as I stared at her face. I was destroyed in that moment. I just watched her fix her mouth to say this to me after she took a day off from work, after she took me home on the train proudly as I held my trophy. She let him take this too. I just nodded to confirm I understood and walked to my room. I thought how I missed Whitney, how none of it even mattered and I just stared out my bedroom window.

That day taught me how fragile joy could be, how quickly it could be stolen, or silenced. But somehow, even after that, joy kept finding me in small, unexpected ways.

5

Permission to LOL

We lived on the 4th floor of an apt building No elevator, two flights of 10 stairs between each floor. They were cold marble tiled floors, Five apartments per floor, each with heavy, metal, burgundy painted, heavy duty pad locked doors. At around 10 years old I would walk home from school and run up from the bottom floor to the top day after day. I noticed it was easier to keep running nonstop and rest later, breathe later.

One day in particular, I noticed a new neighbor had moved in on the 3rd floor. Coming up the stairs, there were 2 doors to the left, 2 doors to the right and one strait ahead. Hers was strait ahead Each day after school about 4 pm. I'd run up these stairs and notice she would keep her door wide open while sitting on her couch which faced the wall of the door, watching sitcoms. I thought to myself, "is she nuts?" Clearly she's not from around here.

At first I was annoyed, as this was an interruption to my painful trip to the top each day. Eventually I got used to it. Eventually,

I looked forward to it then eventually, I barely noticed it. One afternoon on my trip to the top I heard her laughing at the top of her lungs at a show she was watching on television. As I passed her floor, I stopped between the next two flights and I listened. I thought "Did she really just laugh out loud for people to hear?" I'd watch comedies and found some hilarious but would never allow myself to laugh aloud. What If someone heard me? strangely enough It was comforting. Home alone one afternoon, I tried it. I let it out. I was someone else in that moment and perhaps, ever since. It let me know that somewhere this was OK. It was okay to express myself and to be heard. Somewhere anyway, it was okay.

Those moments of laughter were rare, though. For a while, I held on to that small piece of freedom. But home always had a way of reminding me who was really in control, and how quickly innocence could be taken.

6

Sister Sister

One summer during school break, Luther's two daughters from a previous marriage, Terry & Elise, came to stay with us until school started back. It was a very small apartment and there was always someone cramming their way in where ever we lived.

Lauren and I were pretty annoyed but we were polite for the most part. Lauren was very territorial over her belongings and Terry and Elise could not seem to keep their hands to themselves. Our mom taught us to share and be kind but some things were simply off limits. Lauren made that known. If they overstepped, Lauren would let them know she didn't want them touching that. They would shove it back with an attitude and yell "Stuff it!!" We hated that. I found them to be rude which was surprising to me, strict as their dad was.

They came to stay for the next couple of summers. We never looked forward to it but eventually got used to being around each other. We even kind of enjoyed each other's company once in a while. Terry was older than me but younger than Lauren.

She favored Luther and always seemed serious. When she did smile it was pleasant. Elise was younger than Terry but older than me. I was still the youngest. Elise was an absolute Brainiac! So smart and loved to sing but was absolutely not good at it. I don't recall them being very close to him. I could tell they knew him but there was a distance between them.

One afternoon at home with Lauren and our 2 step sisters. Boredom struck I guess. I was the baby of them all so I just wanted to be a part of what ever they allowed me to. It was rare we all got along. One of them suggested we play a game. I don't remember who. "Let's imagine we are with our secret love." Two of us would pretend to be dream guys of the other two and we would be together.

Lauren, the oldest, went to my mom's room with my youngest step sister and I was to go into our room with the older step sister. I didn't quite understand but I knew it didn't feel right. "Who do you want me to be?" She asked me. "What do you mean?" I asked her. She seemed annoyed that I was delaying things. "Who's your favorite star?" she said. So I said Michael Jackson. So she told me to just imagine she was him. She pulled down my underwear and hers and laid on top of me where our triangles touched and she started humping me. She was heavy. I was scared and uncomfortable and Lauren was out of reach. I just kept feeling this wasn't right. I guess she noticed my discomfort and asked me if I wanted to stop and I said yes. So she did. We gathered in the living room after. They were all giggling and I felt sick.

It was never spoken of again, but it left a mark. That moment became one of many that taught me how to shut down and survive. I learned to simply exist through discomfort, to stay quiet when something felt wrong. I didn't realize until much later how that silence followed me, into my relationships, my choices, and my understanding of what love was supposed to look like.

There were still a few people in my world who tried to fill the gaps, to offer me safety, even if only for a little while. My grandmother and Aunt Jasmine became my secret lifelines, the ones who reminded me that I still mattered, even when everything else around me felt unstable.

7

Added Weight

When I was seven, my mother and Luther announced that she was pregnant. It was about to get even more crowded. I started spending a lot of time at my grandmothers. I was always being dropped of there. This was the only place I felt safe anymore. I felt present and loved by my her and by my aunt Jasmine who sometimes lived there.

My grandmother would spend most of the day watching soap operas, murder she wrote and game shows like the price is right. She would smoke cigarette after cigarette all day long. During the commercial breaks she would tell me stories about her life in Jamaica and about my mom, my aunts and uncles growing up. She would repeat the same stories often but it was always just as interesting to hear as the first time. She would make me cornmeal porridge or soft boiled eggs served in the shell. She just had a way about her. A way of doing things and saying things.

My aunt Jasmine would call me her pet. I felt that I was her world.

She would take me places like the museum and the park. She would read to me and tell me I could be anything. She showed me love and attention I hadn't received since before my stepdad entered our lives. She would disappear for moments at a time though. I was never concerned because I knew what a free spirit she was and just figured she was living life and would soon return. She always did.

The next time she returned with a new baby girl who was maybe a year old. I remember being happy but thinking I was no longer going to be her pet. Not because she didn't love me but because there wouldn't be the same time allowed to devote to me. It just wouldn't be the same.

I remember the little girl seemed so unhappy. She didn't smile much like "most little girls". I tried to bond with her. I remember wondering why it was so hard for her to be happy. This little toddler. I remember thinking she was just spoiled.

She ended up growing up very close to us. Tossed from one household to another when my aunt was away. I consider her my sister today. It was later I'd discover my aunt was mentally ill all of this time. She traveled often on the road when she was going through emotional highs and lows as a result of a schizophrenic episode.

The closer it was to our mother giving birth, Lauren would often say "*when that baby comes I want nothing to do with it, I don't want anything to do with anything that is a part of Him!*" I would be like, "Yeah, Me too! Team us!"

As soon as Teresa was born and Lauren saw her face, she melted and team us went to shit. Lauren lived and breathed Teresa whenever she was around. I remember thinking this trifling trader! So much for team us. She was cute but she seemed to cry constantly. When she was asleep she was pretty adorable.

She was so smart. She learned pretty early how to climb out of her crib. They adjusted the crib to raise the bar higher but she was smart and fast and that didn't stop her. Soon she was crawling around dragging things down. Luther had very little tolerance, so even at that young age she was getting spanked on the hands and thighs.

He expressed how disappointed he was that she was lighter skinned and her hair was not nappy enough for his blackness. I should mention my mom is high yellow light-skinned with strait "coolie" Indian textured hair. What was he expecting?

When she started walking and running, she was non stop. The dining room table had a glass top and she would run right under it. As she grew to the height of the table she would still try to run right under the table. I would be sitting at the table and see her coming from my peripheral view and place my hand at the edge just in time to catch her head.

She was always banging that head on something. It was like it was made of steel. I hated it. She would walk right up to me and bang me on my knee with that steel head and I would damn near drop a tear!. Pain like nothing else! She was always getting spanked and when she cried she would laugh. I remember looking at her cry-laughing one day and she was glaring at me, just laughing and crying. I thought to myself, "I don't know about this one."

I learned pretty early that safety was never guaranteed, and just how much the decisions of others could change the course of my day, or even my life.

8

Out of Reach

It was late at night. We would all usually be asleep at this time but we were all up. Mom looked concerned. The window to the courtyard was wide open. Lauren said someone was shot. "Look" she said. I walked up to the window, tip towed and reached to look below from four floors up. Being afraid of heights, I was scared to lean over too far. Lauren held on to my shirt as I leaned over just far enough to see. My feet were off the floor, all except my big toes.

I looked down and there he laid bleeding. In that moment it was like the only color I could make out was the red of his blood. It was not unusual to hear gun shots in our neighborhood. But to see the aftermath of one of those shots was real.

We later learned that our uncle was arrested for his death that resulted from an altercation possibly related to drugs. This was my moms baby brother. It was all around the neighborhood what happened. There was talk about how angry the family of the deceased man was. How at any moment they may retaliate and take out one of his loved ones. Id walk blocks and blocks to and from school each day wondering if this could be the day. Would It be me? My mom? My sister? One of my many other uncles that were stretched out across our street, hanging with their other drunken buddies? What did I know? Kids talk. It eventually simmered down.

For the next several years she lived and breathed my uncle. She did all the footwork to help his case. Her kids, now four of us were on our own to some extent. Lauren was back home and she was mom. And when Lauren was not there, it started to fall on me. When she wasn't in court, meeting with lawyers or visiting baby brother in jail, she was working.

She was always the breadwinner. I don't recall Luther ever working. He went to school for a short while, I believe it was for nursing, but that ended soon after he became disruptive by trying to teach the classes. Soon it became that when I did see my mom, she would walk around with random bruises. I asked her about it once and she told me she ran into a door.

Eventually, the instability at home pushed us farther from Brooklyn, farther from what we knew, and closer to a new kind of uncertainty. Georgia was supposed to be a fresh start, but it brought its own set of challenges.

9

Georgia Bound

My mother became pregnant with my youngest sister soon after my uncle's sentencing. She would visit him regularly in jail. About a year after Nina was born, she sent Lauren and I to live in an apartment in Stone Mountain GA. She was supposed to be out there soon after.

Lauren was 17 and I was 11. The apartment was empty but she sent us food stamps and enough money to buy single mattresses for us to sleep on. It was a two bedroom apartment, much nicer than where we were in Brooklyn but it was empty. We had no transportation so we would often walk to Kroger which was about 6 miles away. It was the nearest grocery store and we would occasionally walk there to pick up groceries or to call our mother when we had minutes on the calling card.

On our first hike to Kroger from the apartment, I was so hot from the sun and tired from the hills. I remember being irritated that my shoes were covered in red dirt and just praying it wouldn't rain. As soon as we could see the Kroger sign at the bend of the shopping center the ground began to level and we got somewhat of a break.

As we were walking along the sidewalk, a blue pickup truck came driving by, there were two white men with dirty blond hair hanging out of the back of the pickup with a cardboard sign with WHITE POWER written on it, yelling "White Power!" Lauren said they spit at us, but I didn't catch that part. I just remember holding Lauren's hand really tight and wondering where on God's green earth we were just sent to live. It was early in the afternoon, bright of day. This was a new kind of hood. We hung out at Kroger for a while then headed back home a couple hours later just hoping we would never see that truck again. We didn't. But we never forgot it.

Soon Lauren got a job at KFC and she was our main support. At some point, our grandmother was sent to live with us and there was a bed put in the second room for her to be comfortable. It was nice having grandma there but she was very elderly and sometimes it was kind of scary being the ones responsible for making sure she was okay.

All of this fell on Lauren. My mom would send us food stamps and they were stretched as far as possible and ends barely met. Lauren's job was paying for most of the rent now and there were times we simply didn't eat. We ate mostly rice and lentil stew because that's what we could afford but even that did not last.

Once, there was an old can of french vanilla slim-fast powder that we got from somewhere and one day, bored and hungry we decided to make a cake out of it. We had flour and sugar and slim fast and baking powder so we made a cake. It was not good. But we had certainly had worse, and there was not a crumb left of it.

I recall one night we were camping out on the living room floor and a co-worker Lauren had confided in, stopped by in the middle of the night after he got off of work to drop off a bucket of chicken and biscuits. It had to be about 2 o clock in the morning, but we all woke up, even grandma, and ate like we hadn't eaten in years.

Till this day I don't remember a better bite of food. We were so grateful. We sat there eating on the living room floor. We put some away for the next day and went right back to sleep. I remember waking up thinking it was a dream. Then it was right back to lentils and rice when we could. We took turns cooking, Lauren and I. I'd often sit with grandma and eat while Lauren was still at work or on a date. Grandma would say, "don't tell Lauren, but I love it when you cook, I'm too old for surprises". It was always way too salty, or way too spicy when Lauren would cook. We never knew which one we would get. But it was always good. We were always grateful.

Now and then Aunt Jasmine would stay with us. But never for long. She was always going where the wind blew her, at least that's how it seemed to me. By now, our relationship was not what it used to be. There was too much going on and I was just more and more stand-offish. I remember she stayed with us during her birthday and Lauren gave her a pair of gold stud earrings with green stones in them.

Lauren always made an effort to give gifts on occasions even when she had nothing. The next morning or maybe a couple days later, I don't really remember, I woke up to Jasmine yelling at Lauren who was also asleep. She threw the earrings at her and started yelling at her "I've only been with two men in my life, and I have no interest in your man!" I didn't know where this came from or where it was going, I just knew I was not waiting around to find out.

I just sat up on my mattress, felt around for my glasses, got up and headed for the front door. I was going to Kroger. I never went alone but I had gone so many times with Lauren that I knew the way. I always dreaded that walk, especially since it was all uphill, but on this day I was here for it.

Lauren saw that I was heading out, which I had never done before, and she shuffled to hurry behind me. I walked and I walked. I didn't know what I'd do when I got there. It's not like I had any money, but I knew I couldn't stay at home. I think we talked on the way but all I remember is her asking me "you okay?", and shrugged my shoulders, but didn't respond.

There was so much I didn't understand back then. Jasmine left soon after, maybe even the same day. When she returned for a quick visit months later, it was like nothing ever happened.

Once she came to visit and brought her daughter, who ended up staying with us when she left again. Eventually, my mother came to visit and she brought Teresa and Nina to stay with us and she left again. I didn't understand why this was happening. One minute, we were moving to GA to be away from Luther and have a better life.

Then over a year had past and it no longer felt like I had a mom. The bond I used to have with my mom before Luther was gone. Lauren did an amazing job of caring for us, providing as best a she could and protecting us but she was not my mom. It was like as soon as Lauren could handle a load without caving, a little more was piled on. I think her only outlet was dating. There was always someone trying to get her attention. We couldn't go anywhere without some man showing interest in her. I found it really annoying. I found her entertaining the attention, even more annoying.

10

Daddy issues

And then there was him, my dad. A figure who existed in the background, a story I wasn't sure I wanted to read. Yet, like all the rest of my life, he came in, not as a hero or villain, but as a person with flaws, forcing me to reconcile what it meant to forgive, accept, and finally see the full picture

When I was about 4 years old, my mom took my hand and walked me down the long dark hallway of our apartment to the front door where a man was standing. He had very big eyes like Lauren and he was holding one of those walk-with-me, toddler-sized Wendy dolls, which was traumatic in itself. "This is your dad." she said.

A man my older sister seemed know fairly well. At four years old I thought, "does this mean there was something missing from my life all this time?" Enduring his embrace and trying match his expression of excitement I'd see him a few times after that.

We lived about a borough apart for most of 17 years and up until my late thirties I think I can count the number conversations we've had together on my hands. He seemed to miss, or pretend to miss the idea that there isn't a bond between us. He'd act surprised that I don't reach out to him or return his "I love you"s. I didn't know this man. What I *did* know, I didn't feel I'd miss.

I knew I had siblings sprinkled around the world over the years, most of whom I'd never met. I recall visiting his side of the family as an adult, with Lauren of course, quiet and watching as he and his siblings reminisced and laughed about the good ole days. They talked about what a ladies man he was and "oh remember when he was engaged to two women at the same time?" I think one of them was my mom, by the way. I resented the idea that I should express artificial love for his benefit.

I no longer blame him because I don't believe he truly knew how to love. As we got older he reached out to me more often, a couple times year sometimes, rarely on a birthday, sometimes through my sister. I'd seldom respond.

A few of years ago, Lauren and I both moved to a small town in Central FL, pushed out by the increasing rents in South Florida. We still lived ten minutes apart. Soon after we moved there she mentioned to me that our Dad bought a house in Florida and is just over an hour away.

She had mentioned his plan to move to FL several times before and just I reassured her, that was neither here nor there, so long as he knows, I don't do drop-in visitors. She would bring him up to me ever so often even when I expressed to her I preferred that she didn't. I tried on many occasions to get through to her that her relationship with him was not the same as mine with him.

She knew him, has lived with him, has experiences with him. Even though they were not primarily the best experiences, they were history that crafted a relationship. I did not have any of this. So it would irritate me that she seemed to expect me to adopt her acceptance of him.

About a year after we were settled. Lauren started saying how old he now was and how she would really like to go visit him to check in. I was in a good place emotionally so I offered, surprisingly, to come along for support... I guess.

She was pretty shocked. I assured her not to get excited. I just wanted to get out of the house and enjoyed a quick road trip. So She picked me up and we headed out. When we got there, it was the same person, but without all the fast talking he usually did. I just sat and watched and listened as they interacted.

They talked about family and memories, my mom, mistakes. He talked about his love for music, how he was, and showed me all the things he built in his home, speakers, furniture, cabinets etc. I knew he was good with cars and that he used to build computers back in the day or something, but I was looking around, and this was not shabby work in the least.

It suddenly seemed there was nothing he couldn't create with his hands. I had never seen this part of him before. The more I watched, I saw me. The only way I could describe it was that as I sat and watched him talk, it was as if Jesus, himself placed his hand on my shoulder and said to me "Let me show you what I see." and I just saw a person in front of me. A person with flaws. Like me.

In that moment, I accepted him as an imperfect person who tried his best with the hand he was dealt. Everyone plays their hand a little differently. We're still not close, me and my Dad, but the resentment is gone and at least our interactions are genuine now. Something in me was set free that day, that I never realized was trapped.

By the time all of this had happened, I was learning how to survive, adapt, and find myself in fragments. Every memory, every person, every heartbreak left pieces of me scattered, and some of those pieces I was only starting to notice were gone.

II

The Lost Pieces

I've pulled from the pieces I could find. Others remain hidden by my own mind, and the thought of what it has protected me from is both frightening and fascinating.

11

Out of Place

I had a really hard time in school. I was quiet and didn't reach out to socialize. Looking back, I think I was just happy to be somewhere other than home. I was shy and awkward. I wore plain sneakers and clothes. As much as I tried to disappear, I stood out like a sore thumb and kids made sure I knew it. They teased me about my clothes, my hair, my glasses, the gap in my teeth, my weight. You name it.

When I first moved to GA, I thought maybe this was a chance to start fresh. New crowd, nobody knew me. Maybe that would be a good thing. But again, I was too quiet, too weird, not cool. There were cliques everywhere. It didn't take long to figure out who was the bully, the popular kids, the followers, and the leaders. I had no interest in any of it.

There was another girl in my class who people made fun of all the time. I felt bad for her, but I also felt guilty for being glad the attention wasn't on me. One day, the popular kid, the school bully known for being the girl who could and would kick a boy's butt, was curiously nice to me. She said, "I just want you to know I'm looking out for you, Tara. Janelle doesn't like you and is planning to fight you after school. If she hits you, what are you going to do?"

I was caught between disbelief and annoyance. I had enough problems already. I just said, "Anyone hits me, I'm going to hit them back." Not long after, I realized they had spun the same lie for Janelle. The whole class was talking about this supposed fight between two of the most unlikely people. Eventually, Janelle came over and said, "Tara, this is stupid. I don't want to fight you and never had anything against you." I said, "Neither do I. I just got here. Friends?" She smiled, "Friends." I remember thinking she was smaller than me yet brave enough to shut it down first. I still admire her for that. We never stayed in touch, but that moment stuck with me.

We had a teacher, Ms. Haney, who was very nice and a great teacher. Ms. Haney was very overweight, and some of the kids were pretty mean about it. At the end of the school year, she said she had a small gift for a few students out of appreciation. She gathered two other girls and me after class and handed each of us a small box.

In the boxes were pretty dangling costume gold and blue ear-rings. I thought, "*it's the thought that counts*", since I didn't have my ears pierced, I was already planning to give them to Lauren. But then I looked inside my box, and they weren't just any earrings, they were clip-ons, the same style as the others but adapted for me. I couldn't believe she really picked these just for me. I felt so seen, so special. I held back tears. That small gesture has stayed with me my whole life.

Even though I felt like a ghost in the halls, moments like the ones with Ms. Haney reminded me that being seen didn't always have to hurt. That little recognition of me, the real me, was rare and powerful. But life had a way of reminding me that being noticed wasn't always safe.

12

Look Both Ways

We moved back to NY after a year or so. Back to the same apartment, back to square one. Winter break was about to start and I had plans to spend it in Long Island with my cousins. It was going to be a welcomed break from the confinement of home. I would be able to celebrate Christmas and see a Christmas Tree again and just be a normal kid for a couple of weeks. If I didn't get anything, it was OK. I was just looking forward to a break.

Coming home from school at the end of the week, I was crossing the final street to my block alongside Lincoln Terrace Park. It was a very busy street and I hated crossing it but I was used to it by now. I looked to the left, looked to the right and rushed forward. I heard a loud boom and found myself thrown several feet to the right.

I was hit by a car coming from the left. My glasses were thrown off of my face and I was laying in the middle of the street, numb. I just knew that if I didn't move I would take the chance of being hit again by oncoming traffic from the other direction.

Everything was in slow motion and sounds were muffled. I could barely see without my glasses.

I found the energy to stand up and limp the rest of the way across the street and leaned against a parked car. Then it was like someone pressed play. Toya, a girl on our block I often walked to and from school with, was walking far ahead of me and I could hear her scream my name and she yelled, "I'm going to get help!" She was pretty fast but I had never seen her run as fast as she did that day.

She ran to get my stepfather and an uncle, I think. Soon there were strange people asking me questions and I was just quiet. I don't remember crying. I just know I couldn't take another step and so I was grateful that God must have lifted me the rest of the way across the street. Soon the ambulance came and took me to the hospital. It was like I had left myself and was just a bystander, barely paying attention.

At the hospital, I just remember laying on the stretcher and random faces appearing above me. My mom, my Dad, a few others. I can't say I was particularly excited to see any of them. I was just going through the motions thinking, "so much for Christmas in Long Island".

But at least I could stay in the hospital. This was even better in some ways I thought. I could use some alone time. I could lay here, watch TV. I even received a few donated gifts that a local charity brought to the hospital at Christmas time. Worked for me!

I was in the hospital for a couple of weeks. I had no broken bones but the muscles in my left hip were completely smashed. I still have a small dent in my hip where I was hit. I recall Toya telling me her father, Mr. G. said, "if she had a little less meat on her bones it would have been much worse".

I was on crutches for another few weeks. I was really pissed that I was now stuck at home with Luther while my mom was at work. Classmates would collect my classwork for me which kept me busy. That, and watching Bob Ross on TV. I usually wasn't able to watch TV but I guess they were easy on me out of sympathy.

When I went back to school, my mom asked my friends to hold my hand while crossing the street and to look out for me. "Great" I thought. I was a little anxious crossing the street after that but I was not about to comply with that request. Soon it was back to life as usual.

After getting hit by that car, I felt a little... untouchable, in a strange way. Not invincible, but alive in a way I hadn't been before. And maybe that was the first time I realized I didn't have to just stay quiet and hope the world didn't notice me. If I could survive that, maybe I could survive saying what I really thought, without apologizing for it.

13

Sorry Not Sorry

One day during lunch period in Junior High, some of the girls and boys decided to play a game of "catch me if you can". This was where the guys would chase the girls and who knows what would happen when they caught them. I wanted no part of it and made it clear that I was not playing and started headed down towards the cafeteria.

A few girls rushed running past me, into the stairwell and right behind them were a group of boys. They were screaming and giggling as they ran by. I pushed my back against the wall as they rushed past, yelling "I'm not playing!, I'm not playing! I'm headed to lunch!"

They all ran past me except for the last boy. This kid was always getting in trouble. No one knew if he was even the right age for the grade he was in. All we knew was that he was not built like an 8th grader. He had big brothers and a dad who would show up at the school when he got in trouble and they all were very muscular and I remember thinking the dad seemed really strict and they all seemed mean.

As he approached me, ignoring my disclaimer that I was not participating in the game, I yelled again, "I'm not playing!" He didn't care and he tried to grab me and missed. I started to run backwards and he leaped to kick me. I grabbed his foot while it was in the air and shoved it away from me, causing him to stumble. I think that may have embarrassed him because he got so upset and immediately punched me in my face.

It seemed to happen in slow motion. The impact was massive. I felt my whole head go numb. But, I didn't cry. It was like something in me took over, getting me through the experience. I did not respond to him. I just looked him in the face and he waited for a second, maybe expecting a reaction, then he ran away. I just stood there for a minute, took a breath and headed down to the office.

When I got there my whole face must have been red and a lady in the office asked me if I was okay. I just sat there and said I wasn't feeling good. I never told anyone. But I decided right then, that would never happen to me again.

Something shifted in me after that. All this time I thought staying in my lane, being kind and sweet would keep me out of harms way. This day that was proved untrue. I started to speak more. I cared a lot less and soon learned that the thoughts in my head had power when I released them.

The following week, a girl who was usually mean and loud was sitting next to me in class. She seemed less on edge recently and on this day, almost friendly. So I said to her, "you know Tanisha, I used to hate you. You were mean and bitchy for no good reason." She looked me in the eyes as if she could not believe I just had the nerve to say that to her. Then she laughed and said "wow, tell me how you really feel." We never had an issue again.

I was a natural at brutal honesty and sarcasm and I was always packing some. I would make people laugh and even hurt a few feelings if I felt someone earned it. I was now the underestimated quiet girl whose words would cut like a knife if you tried her. It was like I gained a level of respect, just by telling the truth, truths I was raised to believe were unkind. But the world was unkind, and I no longer cared.

Learning to speak my mind gave me a kind of armor I didn't have before. But even with that armor, there were still moments that made me freeze in place, moments where I had to trust my instincts and rely on no one but myself. Some situations tested me in ways that even my new sarcasm couldn't fight.

14

Funny Tape

I came by to visit Toya one day after school and Mr. G answered the door. I spent a lot of time at their place when I wasn't at home or at Grandma's. He said "hey Tara!, she went with her mom to the store but they'll be back in a little while if you want to wait." This wasn't that unusual. I went to the living room and sunk into the comfy corner chair. I kept my over-sized jacket on and zipped. I always kept my jacket on even if it was warm. I think it made me feel covered.

Anyway, as I was waiting for her to come home, Mr. G started to make small talk. He told me I could go get something to drink if I wanted and reassured me that I could make myself comfortable. He went into the room to the right of where I was sitting which was the master bedroom. As many times as I had been to that small apartment, I don't recall ever stepping foot in that room.

Soon after, he peeked back out and looked at me. I remember something felt a little off. He said, I'm about to watch a movie if you want to watch with me while you wait. It's a funny tape. I just froze. I had never had a strange feeling around him before and today was different. I replied, "nope I'm okay, but thank you" and offered a polite smile in hopes to convince him that I didn't catch on to what he meant. He smiled back and said, "you sure?" I said "yep, but thanks."

In that moment all I could think of was how I would escape this if things went left. I didn't want to run out or leave abruptly because I didn't want him to think I was going to go tell. I figured that might make him scared or angry. I played the escape route out in my mind over and over but it always came down to: even if I could make it to the front door, I never could get that metal pole lock to work, and I probably wouldn't get out. I always had to have someone else do it and if I struggled trying to *escape*, things could escalate. So I sat there, quiet and still, waiting.

Maybe twenty minutes or so had passed and I heard keys shuffling at the front door and Toya and her mom were back. I was so grateful for the normalcy that was returning to this situation. Mr. G acted as normal of course, and left shortly after. I went into the kitchen to sit with Toya. I told her what happened and she was in shock. She immediately said "Oh my God Tara, he made a pass at you!" She glared at me laughing nervously and in disbelief. Her mom walked in and she told her. Her mom looked at me, silent. I could tell that perhaps she believed me but just had no idea what to do with that information. It was never brought up again, and I never told anyone else.

Even after that, I didn't let fear take over. I started noticing the things I could control, the things I could pour myself into, like my art. Drawing became my way to make sense of everything, the chaos, the trauma, the gaps, and to claim a little piece of life that was just mine. By the time I hit high school, I wasn't just surviving; I was starting to find the parts of myself I wanted to protect and grow.

15

The Constant

My love for art continued to grow. I especially loved to draw people. I seemed to escape when working on a piece. In every drawing, there was something that inspired me, and a clear goal. I would notice that if I rushed, or if I followed someone else's vision, I would end up unsatisfied with the result. It would always seem to impress someone else but I could clearly see where I went wrong and it would bother me.

I had teachers in elementary and Junior High school who encouraged me to pursue art. It was my favorite time in school. I didn't make friends easily. I had thick glasses, crooked teeth and no sense of style. I was teased a lot and the only time anyone seemed to have anything nice to say was when they saw that I could draw. It was the one thing that kept me grounded and people kind of let me be when I was working on a my art which I appreciated.

In public school we were zoned to specific schools depending on where we lived. In my final year of Junior High, one of my teachers encouraged me to apply to a technical High School called Art & Design. My grades were okay, but not the greatest, so I did not get my hopes up.

With my teacher's help, I applied and I had to go to an interview in Manhattan, show them some artwork and I think there was a test of some sort as well. I got accepted and I was really excited. I was no longer bound to the circle I had known. I'd be riding the train to school every day and working toward something. I wasn't particularly excited about meeting new people per say, but I was excited for a change in options.

We had to choose a major in this school and so my major was Fine Arts. I had hit the Jackpot! I get to draw all day. "I got this!" I thought. I soon noticed that while I was "built for this", here, I didn't stand out compared to some of the artists around me. The surrounding talent was remarkable! I was great but surely not the greatest. It was humbling.

I was a part of a much bigger world now, but still really enjoyed it. That is until the Art classes were over. Before I knew it, computers were taking over and graphic design was all the rave. We learned how to use software like Adobe Photoshop, QuarkXpress and all that Mac computers can do. As exciting as that was to many of the students, I missed the pencil to paper, the cray pas, pastels, the charcoal, the paint and the brushes, and I simply could no longer connect. I did okay for a while but I lost interest which led me to find interest in other things that were less productive, like boys, smoking & even drinking.

I met my best friend in High School. Even to this day she is my favorite person. I told her recently she is the George to my Seinfeld for sure. When I first met Linda, we were in gym class. Well, we kind of were anyway. I did my best to steer clear from physical activity, when I could. If a ball went up in the air on the other side of the court I was already ducking so I figured it was in the best interest of everyone, for me to bow out.

I had to be excused to have permission to sit out so I always played the "I have cramps" card with the gym teacher. He knew we were faking most of the time but who had the patience, I guess. Anyway, Linda was sitting out gym that day as well. She was in a grade ahead of me but gym classes usually included a few classes at once.

We were sitting in a hall alongside the gym where students had to go if we were not participating. There were a few other kids there too. I was waiting out the class period, waiting for the bell to ring and Linda chose to sing, very loudly to pass the time. Not a note on key and not a care in the world. "She was getting on my last nerve!" was an understatement.

I'm sure I looked at her, or at least in her direction with loaded looks of "please shut up", but still, not a care in the world. This repeated for several weeks. I don't know how, but eventually were were singing together, laughing together and there was just no shaking this girl. I was happy around her. Not only that, but I was my absolute self around her and still happy, accepted, and never judged. I could tell her the truth good or bad and vice versa and she remained my person. I am to this day, grateful for her friendship, for our sisterhood. We were a recipe for many small disasters and bad choices, but we always had each other's back and we always made it out by God's grace. We shouldn't have survived some of the things we did, or some of the people for that matter.

As close as I felt to Linda, When I decided to move back to Georgia after High School, I had basically cut my losses. In my mind, I figured "I really enjoyed our time together and will never forget her, but bye!" That's just life. Seasons. Change. So we hung out for a bit before I headed of to Georgia and I figured, new start.

The next day I made it to Georgia and she called me and I remember thinking "Oh, we're still doing this?" Day after day, she still called me regularly, like I was still in New York, asking me things like? "Is there a lot of grass in Georgia?" "Are there lots of trees where you live?" She would say "I'm watching Xena Warrior Princess. Do they Have Xena in Georgia?" I could do nothing but laugh, reassuring her that I am not on Mars, just in Georgia. Before I knew it, it was like I never left.

These days, sometimes almost a year might go by without us ever speaking, which is way too long, but when we do reconnect its like we never missed a beat. We'll get on the phone and talk about how God actually trusted us with children. Shortly after our daughters graduated high school she said to me, "can you believe our kids are adults?" I just responded, "Can you believe we're adults?"

High school was a place where I could start to put the pieces together, or at least hold onto some sense of self. But even as I thrived in art, in friendships, in moments of laughter, there were still gaps, holes in my story I didn't understand. And sometimes, those holes would whisper at me in quiet ways, through questions, through moments with my own children, that reminded me there were lost pieces of me I had yet to uncover.

16

Hollow Years

When I started writing this book, the goal was to piece together the parts of my life that felt scattered and hold on to what I could remember, so they didn't get lost in the abyss like so many other memories.

Writing about the people I've loved and those who shaped me has been one of the hardest things I've ever done, not just because of the memories themselves, but because seeing them on the page forces me to confront the person I was and the choices I made along the way.

Growing up, I felt alone, misunderstood, and unsupported. I know my parents loved me, they did the best they knew how. However, living that way made me not just tolerant of solitude, but reliant on it. People could be unsafe, and even the few who didn't hurt me, I kept at a distance. If I started to feel safe, I'd self-sabotage without realizing it. And strangely, the disappointment that followed became almost comforting. I wasn't cruel to people, but I never really learned what it meant to receive love. Translating that into loving someone else? That was a whole other story.

For me, "love" was measured by presence. Who showed up, who didn't. Men in my late teens and early twenties "showed up" plenty. Sex became a drug, something immediate, something I craved without understanding why. It had nothing to do with them, it was about me and the need to feel *something*, anything, to fill the void. Afterwards, disgust would follow, at them, at me, and then the cycle would repeat.

For years, I felt like I was trapped in a looping video game I didn't want to play anymore. Love felt like a puzzle I couldn't solve, and when I couldn't fill that void with people, I looked for ways to fill it myself.

By sixteen, I was smoking, drinking, and sleeping around, trying desperately to fill that bottomless pit inside. The world went on, oblivious, so it had to be me, right? One day, I needed something tangible to blame for the pain. I held a butter knife over a stove burner until it glowed and pressed it to my forearm. The relief wasn't about hurting myself, it was about matching the inside to the outside. I would do this occasionally over the next few years, whenever nothing else numbed the pain enough.

By the time I was stepping into adulthood, I was searching for someone who could show me a different path, but often found the same disappointment mirrored back.

17

Love in Measure

When I was around 20, I started dating someone I was working with. It started out casual, but he soon made it clear he wanted more and didn't want me seeing anyone else. I figured, what the heck, we laughed a lot, and I could be myself around him. As time passed, he became distant as I became clingy. We would get back together, break up, repeat. I still saw him as one person who hadn't hurt me, so I kept him around.

He constantly accused me of flirting, even when I wasn't, while he was flirtatious with everyone. It was hurtful, frustrating, and confusing. I have always believed cheating should end a relationship, and being accused of something I wasn't doing made me lose hope for a future with him. Eventually, brutal sarcasm became my shield once again, a way to endure him without feeling broken.

We ended things, but six months later, I discovered I was pregnant. That's right... six months pregnant and was so oblivious. The shock was immense, but also strangely grounding. I felt, for the first time, a sense of purpose. My daughter's arrival brought the fullest my heart had ever felt, and I hardly dated after that. I had a couple of fleeting encounters, but I quickly realized dating was a distraction from what mattered. By now, I had also become good at turning off my emotions, protecting myself.

Four years later, I had my son. I dated his father for six months. I missed having someone around, but love was never really part of it. He moved in, I became pregnant again, and the pattern repeated: I felt nothing romantically, but knew the practical steps I needed to take. He was unreliable, lied, and drank, and I eventually orchestrated my escape. My kids never met another person I dated after him until over a decade later.

During my second pregnancy, I struggled with the fear that I had already given all my love to my daughter. I thought "could I love this new baby without taking from her?" It was a technical, misconstrued interpretation of love, but I survived, worked, and mothered while feeling numb.

In all these experiences, I was learning the hard way what it meant to protect my heart and prepare for the real work of loving someone beyond myself. That work would begin in a new form when I became a mother for the second time.

After my son was born, I learned how to juggle two children and stay extremely busy. I started school and a new job just six weeks after he was born. By then, I had moved back home with my mom and younger sisters, and the combination of family support and busyness kept me going.

Motherhood was a constant balancing act, an emotional, physical, and mental challenge, but it was also the most grounding experience I've ever known. Through all the chaos and lessons, I began to see that the pieces I had been gathering, my mistakes, my resilience, and my love, were leading me somewhere. They were leading me toward wholeness.

18

Motherhood

I haven't done everything right. I won't do everything right. But God has kept me repeatedly throughout my life through things that I should not have survived. Some things were beyond my control due to the decisions of others, and some due to my own poor decisions.

My first time having a kid was, well... my first time having a kid! And my second time having a kid was, well... my first time having two kids! I do the best that I can to push myself into being a better version of myself everyday in hopes to guide my children into being the best versions of themselves. But I'm working with what I know, just as my parents were working with what they knew.

We have more resources today than they did decades ago so we "should" be doing better, but that's not the case. Now things are harder and add to it, we are now accustomed to expecting instant gratification. And if we could not be gratified before, well... And with the expectation and demand of instant gratification comes great disappointment anger and dismay.

I've never been married and I no longer desire to be. There was a time when it was "the dream" to find the love of my life and be married and be the best wife. But the dream sold in princess movies didn't play out in the lives around me, nor in mine. The true princes are few and far between and for even them, many women are not healed enough from the damage done by the others to trust in them.

Side note: I too "chose the bear". Is there any wonder why? after decades of bears being sold to little girls as a representation of comfort, security and protection? Think about it... Teddy Bears, Care Bears, Yogi Bear, Baloo, Smokey the Bear, even Teddy Ruxpin and I could go on for days... But I digress.

Anyway, for years I'd work and work and when I'd get paid I give it all away and am still in the negative or in debt which ever makes you feel better to say, unable to save. Each year, paid a little more just for prices to increase leaving me almost farther behind and deeper in debt.

I put my life dreams on hold to focus on my role as a mom because I have had to learn what I can handle, and I want them to have the best parts of me rather than waste it on those that have not proven worthy of the time.

Even that has not been seamless. Trying to work more just to make ends meet worked for a while but my kids didn't really have me present. I found myself resentful at times, because loving like a mother is heavy and the older they got the less I could control. I would remind myself in those moments that they didn't choose me and I was most certainly blessed with being their mom.

I've barely traveled anywhere and I have dreams that I am now chasing the clock for without a clear way in sight. Looking back, I think at times that I used motherhood as an excuse for failure. I am grateful that by God's grace I have not endured more than I have. And while I may have been over protective of my kids all these years, I am thankful that they did not have to endure many of the things that I had to go through.

19

The Rabbit Hole

Life had finally settled into a rhythm work, school, motherhood. To everyone else, I seemed fine, maybe even strong. But stillness has a way of stirring what you thought you'd buried. Beneath the routines and the smiles, something inside me was starting to cave in. The hole I thought I'd filled had only changed in shape, and before long, I was slipping right back into it.

One day when my daughter was about 10 years old, we were in the kitchen and she was telling me about the day she had with her dad. He had just brought her home from spending the weekend with him. She was telling me about the loud noises he made when he eats chicken wings. I told her I remember all too well and we laughed. I said "back when I dated your dad"... then she stopped me mid-sentence and her eyes opened up really wide. She looked at me in disbelief and I quickly stopped talking. I was just curious as to what had her so flabbergasted. She continued to say, "YOU DATED MY DAD?!!!" my jaw dropped and I laughed so hard. "Yes", I responded, "I dated your dad and that's how you're here."

In that moment it hit me. She didn't know. She doesn't know... where babies come from or what sex is. Sex, what it is, how it looks and feels, is learned. So how is it that I seemed to have always known? I remembered knowing, as far back as three years old. But that's all I remember. What was I to do with that?

I hid my brief disappearance from our conversation and we laughed and talked some more. But that conversation with my little girl, about chicken wings, broke through another layer of the bubble I'd been living in.

I noticed there were many instances where siblings and family members would talk about memories, many of which involved me and of which I had no memory of. I would remember bits and pieces at times but there were definitely gaps. I have very distinct memories from when I was three and and maybe four, but after that there was almost nothing until about seven years old. I have a few memories within that period, of school, but very little outside of that.

For many years I thought that that was the only block in my memory those years between 3 and 7 years old. But I realized later that this happened way into my thirties. And usually around experiences involving my immediate family.

Based on the information that was available to me, the memories I have of very early sexual feelings and knowledge, reveals what I've felt for so long but never faced, that I was taken advantage of at a very young age. Furthermore, I had no idea who it could be. I had blocked out this information so securely that it could very easily be someone trusted around me, someone close to me, or maybe even someone I remained in contact with having no idea. This has had a big impact on my ability to trust people or build close connections.

20

Piecing Me Together

Looking back, it's easy to see the threads of my life, some bright, some dark, some barely visible. The awkwardness in school, the friends I lost, the people who hurt me, the men I loved and the ones I tolerated, the mistakes I made, the heartbreaks, the burn marks I left on myself, the births, and the years of motherhood where I gave everything and sometimes felt like nothing. Each piece felt random, scattered, sometimes forgotten. And for so long, I thought that was just who I was: broken, incomplete, surviving.

But the more I examine it, the more I realize that even the broken pieces have meaning. They taught me resilience I didn't know I had. They taught me boundaries, even when I ignored them. They taught me what I valued and what I wouldn't settle for. Most importantly, they taught me that survival isn't just getting through, it's learning to hold yourself with kindness even when the world hasn't.

At the time, I didn't have a manual for any of it. I had no guide for love, for motherhood, for loss, for myself. And yet, here I am, still standing, still trying, still piecing together a life that feels closer to whole each day. The pieces aren't perfect, and some days I still feel the emptiness or the doubt creep in. But they are mine, and they've brought me to a place where I can finally start to see the outlines of something bigger: a life built on understanding, on intention, on real love, not just for others, but for me.

This is where *The Road to Wholeness* begins. Not because everything is fixed, or because I've solved every problem, or because I've forgiven everyone perfectly. No, It begins because I am willing to see the value in the fragments I've collected, to use them to shape my life consciously, and to keep moving forward, one imperfect, messy, beautiful step at a time.

III

The Road to Wholeness

Before I share what came next on my road to wholeness, I want to honor the little girl who carried me through so much. Writing to her was the first step in reclaiming the parts of me I had long protected, hidden, or doubted. This is my letter to her, the little Tara who held on, even when the world made it hard.

21

Dear Little me

Dear little Tara,

Thank you for holding it down. Thanks for holding my hand and even running out ahead of me to protect me from this big bad world. Especially after all you've put up with. You are so brave! But you're tired and you need rest. I'm all grown up now, so I got this. But before I rock you to sleep there are a few things that I think you should hear that I wish someone had said to you sooner.

First and foremost, you are a child of God.

You are beautiful inside and out.

You are so smart and creative. Don't ever dim that for anyone, ever!

You are valuable and You are no one's inconvenience.

You are not responsible for the happiness or expectations of others.

Genuine love is never for bargain.

Joy is forever yours to keep.

You have a right to be heard and protected.

Some will see the light in you and try their hardest to snuff it out with lies and with harm, but God has a purpose for your life.

He breathed life into you, so don't hold your breath when you are afraid. Breathe it in and know you are never alone.

You have a Heavenly Father who chooses you every day and loves you unconditionally.

Tara, you did great! And I love you so, so much.

I'll take it from here.

22

When Worlds Collide

As the child of a Jamaican family growing up in Brooklyn, finding my footing was always challenging. My mom was a 5' 2", light-skinned, Coolie-haired woman often mistaken for Hispanic until she opened her mouth. I was the spitting image of my mom, except my hair was thicker, and I never seemed to fit in anywhere.

At school, I was not Black enough. I was too meek, too nerdy, didn't dress "cool," too overweight, my glasses were too big, my teeth too crooked. It was always, *"You'd be pretty if..."* I was unacceptable just by showing up.

I'm grateful, though, that I grew up there. That area, along with my mom's guidance, helped me stay aware of my surroundings and resilient. She taught me that the world could be a dangerous place. I'm not going to say she didn't go overboard at times, but now that I'm a mom, I understand more of why she did.

At home and around family, she spoke pure patois. But to anyone outside, a teacher, a utility company, or when she'd take me to the bank, she would switch to this *English* accent that I found repulsive. Not because of the accent itself, but because "*who was this*? And why?" Was it shame? Fear that she wouldn't be seen as intelligent if she spoke her natural dialect?

I always saw my mom, all 5'2" of her, as strong, intelligent, resourceful, and caring. So if this was the side of herself she had to create to feel accepted, why was that? It wasn't until much later, when I moved to Georgia, that I realized the things I saw in movies about cruelty between people, over something as simple and uncontrollable as race or ethnicity, weren't just on TV. I spent the first twenty years of my adult life there. There were good experiences and some pretty crappy ones. What I learned is that we're all just different and flawed.

By then, I had gotten used to the Southern charm, the gentle greetings of strangers. It was quite the culture shock when I first moved there from New York. Back in Brooklyn, if a stranger so much as made eye contact with you in Brooklyn back then, you were about to get robbed, assaulted, or worse. People just weren't wrapped too tight. So you kept it moving.

But it wasn't until moving to South Florida in 2016 that I experienced the culture shock of my life. I dreamed of moving to Florida for years. I had visited a time or two and had never experienced a sky so open and bright. Sunshine, palm trees, beaches, what's not to love?

One morning, driving to work, I stopped at a red light, when I looked over at the grassy median on my left. A landscaper was out there treating it. As I looked closer, I realized he wasn't just treating it, he was painting it a brighter green. I couldn't believe it. The grass was literally being painted. And it ended up feeling so symbolic, because that's exactly how Florida felt to me after a while, bright and beautiful on the surface, but not always what it seemed. The grass really isn't always greener on the other side.

I was not prepared for the culturally ignorant interactions I would have. And I take responsibility for some of the ignorance as well, because "what was this?" I thought. People were cold, rude. The comments to my face from co-workers would have me stunned. There was a lot of "nice-nasty" wrapped up as southern charm.

For the first year, I cried often. I couldn't understand why people were so rude and mean. I'd look around at this beautiful place and think, "*how could they be so mean-spirited in a place like this?*"

I thought I was prepared, I was born and raised in Crown Heights, and raised by Jamaicans. I was used to people being very direct, but not really *rude*. It wasn't everyone, of course, but many of the uncomfortable moments came from white people. What hurt even more, though, were some of the lighter-skinned Hispanics who seemed even more dismissive, almost competing for approval from whiteness by distancing themselves from what looked different. Again, not everyone, but enough to notice a pattern.

At work, my natural hair often captured the attention of non-

Black people. My hair would be petted. I was asked things like, "Do you know how to braid?" Once, my boss's mother, an older white lady, smiled and said, "You're so kept together... do you do your own cleaning?" as if she was waiting for me to say yes so she could offer me an "opportunity." It would have been different if the other women I worked with, Hispanic and white, were asked the same kind of questions, but they weren't.

I recall taking my kids to the beach one day with my sister and her husband. On our way back to the car, we stopped at an ice cream truck to cool off with a few icees. The truck had a bright Cuban flag painted on the side, and the man inside, maybe in his fifties or sixties, smiled faintly as I placed my order for three ice pops. When he told me the total, it seemed higher than what was listed on the menu. It wasn't a huge difference, but money was tight, so I asked him to confirm the prices. He looked me dead in the face, gestured to his arm, and said, "Those prices are for us."

For a second, I thought I must have misunderstood. But I hadn't. My heart sank. I just nodded and ordered two for the kids instead. Walking away, blood boiling, I tried to make sense of it, how someone could make that kind of distinction over something as simple as ice cream.

"Where was I?" And what's worse... the few times I tried to share how I felt with people who had seen or experienced the same things, it was brushed off with, "Yeah, that's just how it is here." How could a place so bright and warm feel so cold?

Of course, bias and ignorance exist everywhere. But here, it felt layered in a way I hadn't experienced before, hidden behind smiles that didn't quite reach the eyes. I think that God put me here for a reason though. I found a church home that poured love into me where I needed it most, as a person needing community, guidance in my faith, and just hope as a mom, and as someone who needed healing.

I joined a women's life group, which I am still a part of today. There were moments where I would go to group and sit and think, "*I just want to feel in the world, the way I feel in this room.*" It saddened me because, did I feel this way because the people in this building chose to put on their best personality only in this space? Did I feel these people were safe merely in comparison to what's outside?

I struggled with this for a while. It was a me issue. It's hard to know who to trust when I can't even rely on the information my mind has protected me from. How does one get close to people with a mind like mine? I just don't know what I don't know. It's one of the reasons I am so fascinated by people, the good, the bad, and the ugly.

23

Good Grief

By the time Aunt Jasmine got sick, I thought I had mastered the art of keeping it together. I didn't realize that grief was the one emotion I couldn't out-think."

When I learned that Aunt Jasmine was diagnosed with Stage four cancer. I did what I usually did when Lauren delivered *uncomfortable* news. I filed it in the "processing" folder in my brain and went into "keep functioning" mode.

Lauren was often the bearer of bad news. I was usually the last to know anything and when I did learn about something she was often the messenger. Looking back I think perhaps she was pushed into the role of "keeper" over her siblings and never did shake it. That, and she was the only one who felt near enough to me to push through my strict "do not call" policy and my resting-bitch-face.

I learned about Aunt Jasmine on a Sunday. I plowed through my tasks for the day and when I laid down for bed that night

I thought of how I was going to explain this to the kids. I may not have spent much time with her in recent years but she was always around whenever anyone needed her. To babysit or to visit and she often helped out with watching the kids when they were very young.

Aunt Jasmine was great with kids. Just like she was great with me as a kid. Even when she wasn't around, she was thinking of you. We would get birthday cards in the mail for the kids when she was far away. Or we would randomly start receiving a subscription in the mail to some magazine with a topic we had interest in.

Anyway, I thought of a co-worker who just lost a close friend to cancer and she shared how hard it was on her kids and family. Even though her kids were much older, I figured, I'll ask her for some advice when I go to work in the morning.

The next day I walked into work and sat at my cubicle and when the day started, I headed over to my co-worker and I started to bring up what was on my mind. I got as far as "I thought of you yesterday, because I could use some advice on how to talk to my kids because... So I found out this weekend that my Aunt Jasmine has Stage Four Cancer" and just as that last word left my lips, I broke down into tears.

I felt, once again, completely caught off guard and I tried to assure her and an on-looking co-worker that I was fine and I had no idea how or why I started leaking from my eyes, explaining it as an obvious malfunction. "Ewe! What was happening?!" I thought. Whatever it was, it was not acceptable. I started apologizing as they just looked at me with the grossest concern, assuring me it was okay to feel. "Whatever! Never mind" I said. I had work to do. I just thanked them and dove into the day's tasks.

Having this new information about Aunt Jasmine, did not lead me to reach out to her anymore than before. If anything, it made it harder. Many months later, Lauren again... mentioned to me that Jasmine was getting worse and was in the hospital again. I called my cousin on face-time who was with her in the hospital and she turned the phone to Aunt Jasmine. She was pale and all of her hair was gone. Jasmine had the most thick and beautiful hair for as long as I could remember. The person looking back at me was someone else.

When she saw it was me on the phone, she greeted me and I put a smile on my face but if there was anyone who knew me, it really was her. She saw right through my smile and probably figured "if Tara's calling me, my pet must be scared." She instantly said to me, "it's okay Tara-lee!", as she put on a similar smile, "Tara I'm fine and it's okay." I could barely speak and try to control the concern in my face at the same time so I just held back the tears and smiled and said "I know Aunt Jasmine, I love you." All I could think was she is on her death bed and still concerned about me. I was disgusted with myself and very unsettled.

Not long after that, maybe a few weeks or so later, I was headed out to have dinner with a couple of friends and just as I was pulled into my parking spot I saw a call from Lauren coming in. It was rare that I would answer my phone back then. I usually screened calls. It was like I needed to prepare myself for what the world might be trying to inflict on my personal space. But I knew in my soul what this call was about and I was not about to answer.

I then received a text message. I thought there's no way I'm looking at that text or calling her back right now. I knew I needed to go inside the restaurant and immediately order a strong-ass margarita and I did just that. Drinking my margarita as I waited for my friends, I read the message that said " Jasmine's gone." I went on to have dinner with my friends. I mentioned I had a hard day but didn't say why until the end of the night. This too would be filed, and I would go into task mode the next day.

Over the next couple of days I received the funeral details and I was planning a flight to make it there. The funeral was taking place the same week that I was to be serving at a week long Youth camp with our church. The kids were both attending and I figured I would get settled there, leave to catch a flight and head back there to finish out the week with them.

My daughter decided she wanted to go with me so we left my son at the camp with his group and caught a flight from FL to GA and we stayed at my mom's. I was pretty accepting of why we were there. Aunt Jasmine was no longer suffering and I felt a peace for her. Similar to when I lost my grandmother decades earlier.

She was in a better place. The next morning, we rode to the funeral with my mother and younger sister. The car ride there was joyful and I remember it was lighthearted and we laughed and sang along to a worship song that had recently come out,

Holy Water. I loved that song. It was a beautiful morning.

As we pulled up, I could overhear family conversations disputes and just family being family I guess, which made this even more like just another day. As we entered the Catholic church where the funeral was held, I walked down the isle and looked straight ahead at a huge picture of Aunt Jasmine that stood at the front.

Instantly I was unsettled and confused. My hearing became muffled and I felt like the room was caving in. I looked around at everyone there and I remember even looking back at the entrance as if to ask myself how I got here. I was prepared to say goodbye to Aunt Jasmine, who I had spoken to on face-time a while back but that's not what this was.

The picture of Aunt Jasmine that was posted was the Aunt Jasmine to four-year-old me. I didn't come to say goodbye to her. I never would. The whole world around me seemed to crumble and I was inconsolable. So much so I was embarrassed. This was not me. People tried to console me and I could not seem to get a grip. I was sitting next to my mom and I was so ashamed. I looked over at her and she was so collected, not a tear, on the outside anyway. She wouldn't even look at me. I can't imagine how she was handling things. She had also lost a brother the week prior. Two siblings a week apart and here I was a blubbering mess in a Catholic Church no less.

We made it to the end of the service which is still a blur to me and I couldn't make it out of there fast enough. I headed outside to continue my cry, still wondering why no one told me we were saying goodbye to Aunt Jasmine today. She was gone.

My daughter and I headed back to FL and somehow she contracted COVID so we couldn't go back to the Youth Camp. I tested negative but here we were back in the trenches. I had my daughter to care for. I had to prepare to move out of town in less than two months and had no idea where I was moving to. Money was tight as usual and the one thing I looked forward to, my church, I would be saying goodbye to soon as well because I was being priced out of the area I was renting in.

I was so heartbroken on so many levels and there was no time to deal with my grief. I was like an open wound for months and everything was hard. I just wanted to go back to not feeling, to having some sense of control, at least over myself if nothing else. But I was losing my grip on all of it.

24

Where Healing Begins

For the first time in years, I could no longer hide behind walls or tasks. I had to face the feelings I'd spent a lifetime avoiding, and that's when the real work of healing began.

When you've mastered the art of numbing for as long as I have, it becomes both a blessing and a curse. On the one hand, there was always an out when I needed one. But I've learned that building up a wall not only kept bad things out it kept out a lot of good.

I was so used to not feeling, not showing emotion. Not having to face reality when life became too much. But when I became a mom, something cold in me broke off instantly. Reality shifted. I began to feel again, whether I wanted to or not. Trying to go back to the numbness was like grabbing for melting ice.

I knew I wanted to feel better. To be better. To become the best version of myself, the best mom. But I had no idea how grueling the process of re-association would be.

They say therapy is like peeling an onion: layer after layer until you reach the core. The closer I got to the core, the more vulnerable I became. I felt like an open wound, hurting inside and out. I was constantly bursting into tears over what seemed like nothing. I felt so foolish. But I was feeling everything.

I've always had a heightened sense of awareness for just about everything around me. In fact I believe this motivated me even more to become so good at dissociating. But it is a completely different thing to really feel it all.

It was hard enough seeing myself that way. But seeing the reactions of those who "knew me", their faces filled with concern, as if to say "Welcome back" made it worse. It felt well... gross. It became more difficult to stifle out the feeling so I leaned on unhealthy connections, alcohol, work. Anything that would keep me busy enough to lose myself in it became my vice. I had no sense of control anymore.

Eventually, many years later, I leaned in, despite hating so much of it, because I knew there was no turning back. I was making everything worse and my kids deserved a better version of their mom.

Losing control pushed me deeper into needing the presence of my Heavenly Father. I needed someone to hold me up through the hurt. I needed Him to see me through. I still do.

25

Boundaries and Grace

For many years, I was deeply resentful toward my mom. I spent a good decade loving her only in theory, acknowledging that she was my mother, but feeling very little toward her. From my teenage years through my early twenties, I was emotionally shut down with her. It was easier to say very little and just do what needed to be done.

She lived and breathed my younger sisters and everything they had going on. If you weren't on board, in line, or available to help manage their needs or the needs of anyone else she chose to save, you were essentially on your own, or even in the way. Because of that, I moved away often, sometimes cities away, determined to create and maintain distance.

But almost every time I left, I found myself circling back. I'd move out of her house, only to spend time still under her roof. It was like I needed space, yet still needed her presence. Even when I was miserable, I wanted to be near her. That contradiction frustrated me more than the distance itself. I couldn't understand why I wanted away and closeness at the same time.

It bothered me that my siblings had constant contact with her, but I learned to cope by telling myself this wasn't the mother I remembered. My older sister was always the pursuer, the fixer, the one who maintained contact with our parents. I wasn't. My younger sisters felt entitled, disrespectful and demanding. There were long stretches, even into recent years, where I barely spoke to my mom. When she did call, it was often to check on someone else.

There were times when I really just needed my mom, and I didn't know how to ask for that, or believed it would make a difference. When I had children, she was very present, sometimes overbearing, full of opinions about how things should be done. In the early years, when I was emotionally and financially unstable and living with her at times, I tolerated it out of respect. Still, it hurt. There was so much concern for others when I needed it most as her child.

Maybe that's something you don't fully understand until you're a grandparent. Just like there are things I didn't fully understand until I became a parent myself.

Over time, I realized it was on me to grow up in a different way, to accept that my mom did the best she could with what she had. I also realized that from the outside, my quiet looked like strength. I didn't complain. I didn't demand. I didn't ask. So it probably appeared that I had it handled, while others were more vocal about their needs, their anger, their pain. But that quiet isn't the kind of strength I want anymore.

Now that my kids are older, my relationship with my mom has changed. She listens to me. She cares about what I think and how I feel. Sometimes I wonder if she would have back then, had I spoken up, but there's no way to know. What I do know is that she now tells me she's proud of the job I've done raising my kids and working on myself. At times, she even seems inspired by it.

It makes me want peace for her. Rest. A life where she doesn't feel responsible for saving everyone. I forgive her. But forgiveness doesn't mean going backward. My boundaries, with her and with my family, are clear. I won't tolerate what no longer fits the life I'm praying for.

If there's one thing I've learned in life, it's that you teach people how to treat you by what you're willing to endure. For a long time, my silence did the teaching for me.

There are still moments when my mom slips back into old patterns, especially when it comes to not setting boundaries with others. In those moments, I let go. Because mom or not, I won't be dragged back into a place I fought my way out of.

That doesn't mean I love her any less. It means I'm committed to the version of this relationship we've built now. One that doesn't live in what should have been, but in who we are today. No steps backward.

Things are good now. And like any relationship, it is what it eats.

26

Triggers & Transformation

Even as I leaned on God and tried to keep it together, I realized His work in me wasn't done. There were still rooms of my heart I hadn't even opened, doors I wasn't ready to face, and feelings I'd been avoiding for years, just waiting to show up.

Every so often, I feel like I've plateaued. I reflect on my healing journey and see how far I've come. But then, out of nowhere, something new sticks out like a sore thumb. Another issue. Another layer to address.

For me, inner work is like cleaning house. It's always easiest to notice when something's out of place after the house is clean. Whether it's spring cleaning, a quiet day off, or just tidying up after the kids, back then or even now that they're older, once the house is in order, anything out of place stands out right away. A sock on the floor, a dish left on the counter, those things are easy to catch when the space is already clean.

But when I let things go, when the laundry starts piling up, when people come and go without pause, and the toys, socks, and random items get tossed around, then everything starts to blur together. It's not just one thing out of place. It's all a mess. The clutter becomes normal, and it's harder to notice what needs attention. That's what unhealed pain can feel like.

It's as if my life is a huge, old house with many rooms. Some are my favorite spaces, well-lit, familiar, high-traffic areas where I spend most of my time. But then there are those rooms that don't get much attention. They're dusty. Some are swollen shut. Others are locked and bolted, sealed off from the light.

When I'm going through something difficult and start examining my reactions, I've learned to look within. Sometimes, it's easy to trace my response to a clear reason. I can connect the dots between what I'm feeling and where it came from. Other times, it feels like I hear one of those old locks pop open.

Suddenly, I'm aware of a room I hadn't considered. Depending on where it is in the house, I might be willing to explore it, shine a light, dust off the corners, maybe even realize there was no monster in there after all. But if that room is tucked away in an area I usually avoid, I'm faced with a choice:

Do I go in and explore while I'm awake, aware, and strong enough? Or do I ignore it and risk that whatever is in there will find its own way out? Roaming the halls of my life unnoticed. Shadowing my days. Showing up when I least expect it. Ready or not.

I remember in the beginning stages of my therapeutic journey,

I was finally starting to get the hang of it, or at least I thought I was. The sessions were helping, I guess. They made sense to me, and I was starting to find some purpose in the process.

One morning, I had a therapy appointment scheduled. Everything was going smoothly. The kids were up and ready on time, I dropped them off at school, and I was actually early for once. I even had enough time to swing by a drive-thru and grab a coffee so I could be relaxed and focused for my session.

As I pulled out of the drive-thru, coffee in hand, I remember thinking, I'm actually doing pretty good. I really don't have anything I need to talk about today. I guess we'll see. I got to my appointment, signed in, and sat down on my therapist's couch. She smiled and said, "So, how are we doing today, Tara?"

I said, "I'm good. I mean... I've got nothing. I don't really have anything on my mind today" Then I opened the little sip flap on my to-go cup, took a sip, and it was tea. Not coffee. Instantly, the tears started pouring down. I was blubbering so hard you'd think something major just happened. Turns out, I had a lot more to get off my chest than I realized.

When I don't tend to myself regularly, it all builds up. And when I finally do face it, it feels overwhelming, not impossible, but heavier, more exhausting, and a much bigger task to begin.

27

My Superpower

Early this morning I watched a clip from The Sherri Shepherd Show where she had Henry Winkler on. She shared how, the first time she appeared on Hollywood Squares, she was so nervous.

She wasn't as well-known as the other celebrities, and during lunch she looked around and saw everyone chatting in their little groups, while she sat there alone, feeling out of place. Then she said Henry came and sat next to her. And as she was telling that story, she started tearing up. And so did I.

And right as I was about to sarcastically tell myself to get a grip, I was reminded that it's okay to feel deeply. It's okay that I get emotional thinking about someone else's pain, because it's more than sympathy, it's empathy. It's connection.

It also made me think back to the times when I felt like that, alone, unseen, out of place. There were years when I cried almost every day for so many reasons. And then there were years when I didn't cry at all. When I hardened my heart so much that I couldn't feel anything.

But since doing the work, real, internal, spiritual work those feelings have started to come back. Not in chaos, but in clarity. Now, when moments like this hit me, I see them as a gift. It's how God shows me there's something to pay attention to... something to explore.

I've been blessed with a few creative gifts like drawing, painting, baking and writing, all of which I love. But the biggest gift I've been given, the one I used to run from, is empathy. Feeling what someone else feels, even when they don't say a word. Seeing the truth behind a smile because I've worn that same one before.

All the trials, all the trauma, all the years of tears and numbness, they weren't wasted. They've strengthened me so I can show up for others with more compassion, more understanding, and more purpose. I'm done running from myself. As messy, awkward, or quirky as it may look, I'm rolling with it, like I often have. Only now, I'm rolling with intention. And with God's direction.

28

Acceptance

Recognizing my empathy as my superpower made me see not just who I am, but what I'm capable of , and it opened the door to noticing possibilities I'd never allowed myself to consider before.

As I began peeling back the layers and returning to my core, I started to see doors and pathways, opportunities I hadn't noticed before. I found myself drawn to things that once scared me or seemed so far out of reach, I assumed they weren't meant for me. It was confusing at first. I started to doubt myself, wondering if I was just being flaky or indecisive.

But the more I explored, the more I realized, those doors were always there. I just hadn't seen them before. I needed to go through certain experiences to gain the perspective to recognize them. What I thought was indecisiveness was actually discovery.

So yes, it is my right to explore. It is my right to grow, to evolve, and to walk through those doors as they reveal themselves, every single day. And I intend to, fully, boldly, without apology, because this is my life, and I can finally see the view from here.

About the Author

Tara Gardner is a mother, writer, and lifelong student of life. Born and raised in New York City to Jamaican immigrant parents, she holds a BA in Sociology and shares her journey of resilience, faith, self-discovery, and creative expression to inspire others.

Guided by her Christian faith, she is passionate about helping others confront their inner struggles, embrace healing, and find hope through perseverance. When she's not writing or coaching, Tara enjoys creating art, spending time with her children, and finding moments of joy in everyday life.

Made in the USA
Coppell, TX
22 February 2026

71988642R00069